METAWALLAH: THE PRICELESS DEGREE

BREAKING BARRIERS: FREE EDUCATION FOR ALL

PRASHANT PANDEY

Made with ♥ on the Notion Press Platform
www.notionpress.com

"Dedication: This book is dedicated to all those who aspire to learn and grow, regardless of their financial means. May this guide inspire and empower you to access free education and unlock your full potential."

"Author: Prashant Pandey is an educator and advocate for accessible education. With years of experience in the education industry, Prashant is passionate about helping individuals overcome financial barriers to learning. This book is a testament to his commitment to empowering learners everywhere."

Contents

Contents

Foreword

Education is a fundamental human right, but sadly, not everyone has access to it. In the current education system, the cost of education is one of the biggest barriers for many individuals, preventing them from accessing the knowledge and skills they need to succeed. This is a tragedy, as education is the key to unlocking opportunities, expanding one's horizons, and improving one's quality of life.

As someone who has been involved in the education industry for many years, I have seen firsthand the positive impact that education can have on individuals, communities, and societies. I have also seen the challenges that students face in accessing quality education, particularly those from low-income backgrounds. That is why I am so passionate about free education, and why I believe that it is the solution to many of the challenges facing the education sector today.

This book, "Breaking Barriers: Free Education for All," is a comprehensive guide to accessing knowledge without financial barriers. It is a guide that has been carefully curated to help individuals of all backgrounds and levels of education to access the resources they need to learn, grow, and thrive.

In this book, Prashant Pandey, the author, takes us on a journey through the current education system and the challenges that students face due to financial constraints. He then provides a detailed analysis of the different types of free education resources that are available, from online courses to community resources and libraries. The book also includes tips on how to create a self-learning plan, manage time effectively, and acquire new skills that can boost career prospects.

One of the things that I appreciate about this book is the breadth of resources that the author has included. As someone who has worked in the education industry for many years, I know how difficult it can be to find quality resources for free. Prashant has done an excellent job of curating a list of resources that are both reputable and accessible, which will be of great benefit to anyone who is looking to learn without the burden of financial constraints.

Another thing that stands out about this book is the author's commitment to empowering learners. Prashant recognizes that learning is a journey, and he provides practical advice and motivation to help readers stay on course. He emphasizes the importance of setting goals, developing a schedule, and tracking progress, which are essential components of any successful learning plan.

Finally, I appreciate the author's vision for a future where education is accessible to all. This book is not just a guide to accessing free education; it is a call to action for educators, policymakers, and individuals to work together to create a more equitable and just education system. As the world becomes more interconnected, and the demand for skills and knowledge continues to grow, it is imperative that we find ways to make education accessible to everyone. This book is a step in the right direction.

In conclusion, I highly recommend "Breaking Barriers: Free Education for All" to anyone who is looking to learn and grow, regardless of their financial means. The author's commitment to accessible education, coupled with the breadth of resources and practical advice in this book, makes it an essential guide for anyone who is committed to their personal and professional development.

Preface

Education is often seen as the great equalizer, the key to unlocking opportunities and improving one's quality of life. However, in reality, access to education is not always equitable, and many individuals are prevented from accessing the knowledge and skills they need due to financial constraints. This is a tragedy, as it means that many talented individuals are left behind, and the world loses out on their potential contributions.

As an educator, I have seen firsthand the challenges that students face when trying to access quality education. I have also seen the transformative power of education and how it can change lives. That is why I am so passionate about free education and why I have written this book.

The goal of this book is to provide a comprehensive guide to accessing free education in all domains. The book is designed to help individuals of all ages, backgrounds, and levels of education to access the resources they need to learn, grow, and thrive. Whether you are a student, a professional, or someone who is simply interested in acquiring new knowledge and skills, this book is for you.

In this book, I will take you on a journey through the current education system and the challenges that students face due to financial constraints. I will provide an analysis of the different types of free education resources that are available, from online courses to community resources and libraries. I will also provide tips on how to create a self-learning plan, manage time effectively, and acquire new skills that can boost your career prospects.

One of the things that I hope readers will appreciate about this book is the breadth of resources that I have included. I have made a concerted effort to curate a list of resources that are both reputable and accessible, so that readers can be confident in the quality of the materials they are using. I have also tried to cover a range of domains, from STEM fields to the humanities, so that readers can find resources that are relevant to their interests and career aspirations.

Another thing that I hope readers will appreciate is the practical advice that I have included. I recognize that learning is a journey, and that it can be challenging to stay motivated and on track. That is why I have provided advice on how to set goals, develop a schedule, and track progress. I have also included tips on how to stay motivated and avoid burnout, which are important components of any successful learning plan.

Finally, I want to emphasize the importance of accessible education. Education should not be a privilege for the wealthy or well-connected; it should be a fundamental human right. Access to education is essential for creating a more equitable and just society, and for unlocking the potential of individuals and communities. That is why I believe that free education is so important, and why I have written this book.

In conclusion, I hope that this book will serve as a valuable resource for anyone who is looking to learn and grow, regardless of their financial means. I hope that the resources and advice included in this book will empower readers to take control of their own learning, and to pursue their passions and goals with confidence. I believe that by working together, we can create a world where education is accessible to all, and where everyone has the opportunity to reach their full potential.

Acknowledgements

Writing this book has been a labor of love, and I could not have done it without the support of many people along the way. First and foremost, I would like to thank my family and friends for their unwavering support and encouragement. Their belief in me and my work has been a constant source of motivation, and I am deeply grateful for their presence in my life.

I would also like to thank the educators and organizations who are working tirelessly to make free education a reality. Their dedication and hard work are making a profound impact on the lives of countless individuals, and I am inspired by their commitment to making education accessible to all.

I am also indebted to the authors and creators of the many resources that I have included in this book. Their work has been instrumental in helping to create a more equitable and accessible education system, and I am grateful for their contributions to this field.

Finally, I would like to thank the readers of this book. It is my hope that this book will inspire and empower you to pursue your own learning journey, and to believe in the transformative power of education. Thank you for taking the time to read this book, and for your commitment to creating a more just and equitable society.

With gratitude,
Prashant Pandey

Prologue

Education is one of the most powerful tools we have for creating a better world. It has the power to unlock potential, drive innovation, and promote social and economic mobility. However, for far too many individuals, access to education remains out of reach. The high cost of tuition, textbooks, and other materials can be a barrier to entry, preventing many talented individuals from pursuing their educational aspirations.

As an educator, I have seen firsthand the challenges that students face due to financial constraints. I have seen the toll that these barriers can take on their confidence, motivation, and success. But I have also seen the incredible resilience, determination, and creativity that students demonstrate when given the opportunity to learn.

This book is a call to action, a roadmap for how we can create a more equitable and accessible education system. It is a guide to the many free education resources that are available, from online courses and textbooks to community resources and libraries. It is a practical toolkit for anyone who is looking to learn and grow, regardless of their financial means.

But this book is also a celebration of the transformative power of education. It is a reminder that education is not just about acquiring knowledge and skills, but about empowering individuals and communities to shape their own futures. It is a tribute to the educators, creators, and innovators who are working tirelessly to make free education a reality, and to the students who are overcoming barriers and pursuing their dreams.

In the pages that follow, I will provide a comprehensive guide to accessing free education in all domains. I will share tips and advice for creating a self-learning plan, managing time effectively, and staying motivated. I will introduce readers to a range of resources, from MOOCs to Open Educational Resources, and I will highlight the organizations and initiatives that are driving change in this field.

My hope is that this book will serve as a resource and an inspiration for anyone who is looking to learn and grow, regardless of their financial means. I hope that it will help to create a more just and equitable education system, and that it will empower individuals and communities to pursue their educational aspirations with confidence and determination.

Let us begin this journey together, and let us work to create a world where education is accessible to all.

Importance of education

Education is one of the most powerful tools we have for creating a better world. It has the power to unlock potential, drive innovation, and promote social and economic mobility. However, for far too many individuals, access to education remains out of reach. The high cost of tuition, textbooks, and other materials can be a barrier to entry, preventing many talented individuals from pursuing their educational aspirations. This is where Metawallah's free courses come in, offering a way for anyone to gain access to quality education.

Importance of Education

Education plays a critical role in shaping individuals and societies. It provides individuals with the knowledge, skills, and competencies needed to succeed in life and contribute to the world around them. Education is not just about acquiring knowledge and skills, but about empowering individuals and communities to shape their own futures. It is also key to unlocking economic growth and reducing poverty, as well as promoting social inclusion and gender equality.

Education also has a profound impact on health and well-being, with evidence showing that education is strongly correlated with better health outcomes. Educated individuals are more likely to make healthier lifestyle choices, have better access to healthcare, and experience less stress and anxiety. Education also contributes to social cohesion and civic engagement, helping individuals to develop a sense of belonging and connection to their communities.

Role of Metawallah Free Courses

Metawallah is a company that is dedicated to making education accessible to all. They offer free educational courses in all domains, providing a way for individuals to gain the knowledge and skills they need to succeed in life. Their courses are designed to be flexible and accessible, allowing learners to study at their own pace and on their own schedule.

Metawallah's free courses are offered in a wide range of subjects, from business and technology to humanities and the arts. They are created by a team of expert educators, and are designed to be engaging, interactive, and effective. The courses are designed to be accessible to learners of all ages and backgrounds, and are suitable for both beginners and advanced learners.

One of the key features of Metawallah's free courses is the use of technology to create a more interactive and engaging learning experience. They use a range of tools and techniques, such as videos, quizzes, and interactive simulations, to help learners stay engaged and motivated. The courses are also designed to be flexible, allowing learners to study at their own pace and on their own schedule.

The Impact of Metawallah's Free Courses

Metawallah's free courses have had a profound impact on the lives of many individuals. They have provided a way for learners to gain access to quality education, regardless of their financial means. The courses have helped individuals to develop the knowledge and skills they need to succeed in their personal and professional lives, and have contributed to their overall well-being.

Metawallah's free courses have also had a positive impact on the broader community. By providing access to education, they have helped to promote social inclusion and reduce inequalities. They have also contributed to economic growth and development, by providing learners with the skills they need to participate in the workforce and contribute to the economy.

A fundamental human right, and it is the responsibility of all of us to ensure that everyone has access to it. Education is key to unlocking human potential, driving innovation, and promoting social and economic mobility. It is also essential for promoting health and well-being, reducing poverty, and promoting social inclusion.

However, the cost of education can be a significant barrier to entry for many individuals. This is particularly true in low-income and underprivileged communities, where access to education is limited. This is where Metawallah's free courses come in, providing a way for individuals to gain access to quality education, regardless of their financial means.

Metawallah's free courses are designed to be flexible and accessible, allowing learners to study at their own pace and on their own schedule. They are also designed to be engaging and interactive, using a range of tools and techniques to help learners stay motivated and engaged. By providing free access to education, Metawallah is helping to reduce inequalities and promote social inclusion.

The impact of Metawallah's free courses is significant, both for individual learners and for the broader community. By providing access to education, they are helping individuals to develop the knowledge and skills they need to succeed in life. They are also contributing to economic growth and development, by providing learners with the skills they need to participate in the workforce and contribute to the economy.

Education is one of the most powerful tools we have for creating a better world. It is essential for promoting human potential, driving innovation, and promoting social and economic mobility. However, access to education remains limited for many individuals, particularly in low-income and underprivileged communities. This is where Metawallah's free courses come in, providing a way for individuals to gain access to quality education, regardless of their financial means. By providing free access to education, Metawallah is helping to reduce inequalities and promote social inclusion, and contributing to a better future for all.

Conclusion

Education is a critical tool for creating a better world. It has the power to unlock potential, drive innovation, and promote social and economic mobility. However, for far too many individuals, access to education remains out of reach. This is where Metawallah's free courses come in, providing a way for individuals to gain access to quality education, regardless of their financial means.

Metawallah's free courses have had a profound impact on the lives of many individuals, providing them with the knowledge and skills they need to succeed in life. The courses have also had a positive impact on the broader community, contributing to social inclusion, economic growth, and development.

Current barriers to accessing education

Education is essential for individual development and economic growth. However, access to education is still limited in many parts of the world, particularly in low-income and underprivileged communities. In this article, we will explore the current barriers to accessing education and their impact on individuals and communities.

Financial Barriers

One of the most significant barriers to accessing education is the cost. Many families cannot afford to pay for tuition fees, textbooks, and other associated costs. This is particularly true in low-income and underprivileged communities, where families often struggle to make ends meet. The cost of education can be a significant financial burden, and many families have to choose between educating their children and meeting their basic needs.

Infrastructure and Accessibility Barriers

Another barrier to accessing education is the lack of infrastructure and accessibility. In many communities, schools are located far from the students' homes, and transportation is often unavailable or unreliable. This makes it difficult for students to attend school regularly, and many end up dropping out. Additionally, many schools lack adequate infrastructure, such as classrooms, libraries, and laboratories, making it difficult for students to learn and develop the necessary skills.

Language and Cultural Barriers

Language and cultural barriers are also significant obstacles to accessing education. In many parts of the world, schools teach in a language that is not the students' first language. This can make it difficult for students to understand the curriculum and participate in class. Additionally, cultural differences can make it challenging for students to adapt to the school environment and feel comfortable in the classroom.

Gender and Discrimination Barriers

Gender and discrimination barriers also prevent many individuals from accessing education. In some societies, girls are not encouraged to attend school or are forced to drop out to help with household chores. Additionally, discrimination against minority groups can prevent them from accessing education, as they may face harassment and discrimination in the classroom.

Impact of Barriers to Accessing Education

The impact of these barriers to accessing education is significant. Individuals who are unable to access education are more likely to remain trapped in poverty and lack the necessary skills to participate in the workforce. They may also be more susceptible to health issues, as they lack the knowledge and resources to maintain their health and well-being.

Additionally, communities that lack access to education are at a disadvantage in terms of economic growth and development. They are less likely to attract investment and are often overlooked by businesses seeking to expand into new markets. This perpetuates a cycle of poverty, making it challenging for communities to escape.

Role of Education Providers

Education providers play a critical role in addressing these barriers and promoting access to education. By offering flexible and accessible learning opportunities, education providers can help reduce financial barriers to education. Additionally, they can invest in infrastructure to improve accessibility and ensure that schools are located in areas that are easily accessible to all students.

Education providers can also work to address language and cultural barriers by providing language support and incorporating cultural education into their curriculum. Similarly, by promoting gender equality and combating discrimination, they can ensure that all students have equal access to education.

Addressing the barriers to accessing education requires a multifaceted approach, involving a range of stakeholders and strategies. Here are some strategies that can help overcome the barriers to accessing education:

Providing financial assistance: Providing financial assistance in the form of scholarships, bursaries, or loans can help make education more affordable for low-income students. This can help reduce the financial barriers to education, and ensure that all students have the opportunity to access education.

Improving infrastructure: Investing in infrastructure, such as schools, classrooms, and libraries, can help improve accessibility and ensure that all students have access to quality education. This can help reduce the infrastructure and accessibility barriers to education.

Promoting bilingual and multilingual education: By promoting bilingual and multilingual education, education providers can help reduce language barriers and ensure that students who speak different languages have equal access to education.

Providing digital and online education: Providing digital and online education can help overcome barriers related to infrastructure and accessibility, particularly in remote or underprivileged areas. This can help ensure that students have access to quality education, regardless of their location.

Providing cultural education: Providing cultural education can help reduce cultural barriers and ensure that students from different backgrounds feel comfortable in the classroom. This can help promote social inclusion and ensure that all students have equal access to education.

Promoting gender equality: By promoting gender equality and encouraging girls to attend school, education providers can help overcome gender barriers and ensure that all students have equal access to education.

Conclusion

Access to education is a fundamental human right, and addressing the current barriers to accessing education is essential for promoting human development, economic growth, and social inclusion. Financial, infrastructure, language, cultural, gender, and discrimination barriers all prevent individuals and communities from accessing education, perpetuating cycles of poverty and inequality. Education providers have a critical role to play in promoting access to education and addressing these barriers, making education available to all. By investing in education, we can create a better world, one where everyone has the opportunity to learn, grow, and succeed.

CHAPTER THREE

Purpose of the book

The purpose of the book is to promote access to education for all individuals, regardless of their background, economic status, or circumstances. Education is a fundamental human right, and it is critical for individual development, economic growth, and social cohesion. Yet, many barriers prevent individuals and communities from accessing education, perpetuating cycles of poverty and inequality.

The book aims to address these barriers by offering free educational courses through Metawallah. These courses cover a range of topics and domains, from math and science to literature and art. The courses are designed to be accessible to everyone, regardless of their educational background, and can be taken online or in person, depending on the individual's preferences and circumstances.

The book is divided into several chapters, each covering a different aspect of education and its importance. The first chapter provides an overview of the importance of education, highlighting its critical role in individual development and economic growth. The chapter also covers the challenges that prevent individuals from accessing education, such as financial, infrastructure, language, cultural, and gender barriers.

The second chapter covers the role of Metawallah in promoting access to education. It provides an overview of the company's mission and values, and how it is helping individuals overcome the barriers to accessing education. The chapter also covers the different courses offered by Metawallah, and how they are designed to be accessible to everyone.

The third chapter covers the impact of education on individuals and communities. It provides case studies and examples of how education has transformed the lives of individuals, and how it has contributed to economic growth and social cohesion. The chapter also covers the benefits of promoting education and the potential long-term impact of Metawallah's efforts.

The fourth chapter covers the future of education and how Metawallah's initiatives are shaping the future of education. The chapter covers the potential of digital and online education, and how it can help overcome barriers related to infrastructure and accessibility. The chapter also covers the potential of bilingual and multilingual education, and how it can help reduce language barriers and promote social inclusion.

The final chapter provides a call to action for individuals, communities, and education providers to work together to promote access to education. It highlights the role of education in creating a better world and emphasizes the importance of creating a more equitable and inclusive society.

In conclusion, the purpose of the book is to promote access to education and to highlight the critical role of education in individual development and economic growth. The book offers a range of strategies and solutions for addressing the barriers to accessing education and provides an overview of Metawallah's initiatives in promoting access to education. The book is a call to action for individuals, communities, and education providers to work together to create a more equitable and inclusive society, one where everyone has the opportunity to learn, grow, and succeed.

CHAPTER FOUR

Current education system in different parts of the world

Education systems vary widely around the world, with different countries and regions adopting various approaches to education. While some education systems are highly centralized and structured, others are more decentralized and offer greater flexibility. In this article, we will explore the current state of education systems in different parts of the world, highlighting their strengths, weaknesses, and challenges.

North America: Education systems in North America, including the United States and Canada, are highly decentralized and vary from state to state or province to province. While public education is offered to all students, the quality and availability of resources vary widely. Many schools in North America struggle with issues such as inadequate funding, unequal distribution of resources, and standardized testing.

Europe: Education systems in Europe vary from country to country, with some countries offering a centralized approach to education while others opt for a more decentralized approach. In general, education in Europe is considered to be of high quality, with an emphasis on critical thinking, problem-solving, and creativity. However, access to education can be a challenge in some regions, particularly in poorer areas.

Asia: Education systems in Asia are often highly centralized, with a strong focus on academic achievement and standardized testing. Countries like China, Japan, and South Korea are known for their rigorous education systems that prioritize math and science. However, these systems are often criticized for their lack of emphasis on creativity, critical thinking, and problem-solving. In contrast, education systems in Southeast Asia, such as those in Vietnam and Thailand, are often more focused on practical skills and vocational training.

Africa: Education systems in Africa face many challenges, including inadequate funding, poor infrastructure, and a shortage of qualified teachers. Many students in Africa struggle to access education, particularly girls and children from poor families. However, some countries, such as South Africa, have made significant strides in improving education access and quality.

Middle East: Education systems in the Middle East are often highly centralized, with a strong emphasis on traditional subjects such as math, science, and religion. However, there is growing interest in modernizing education systems in the region and placing a greater emphasis on critical thinking, creativity, and problem-solving. Access to education can also be a challenge in some areas, particularly in conflict zones.

Latin America: Education systems in Latin America vary widely from country to country, with some countries offering highly centralized and structured systems while others offer more flexibility. Many schools in the region face challenges such as inadequate funding, poor infrastructure, and a shortage of qualified teachers. However, there is growing interest in expanding access to education and improving its quality, particularly in countries like Brazil and Chile.

While the education systems in different parts of the world have their unique strengths and weaknesses, there are some common challenges that many countries face. One of the biggest barriers to education access is poverty. Students from low-income families often lack the resources and support needed to succeed in school, such as access to books, technology, and extracurricular activities. Additionally, students from marginalized communities, such as those from indigenous or minority groups, may face additional barriers to education access due to discrimination and social exclusion.

Another major challenge facing education systems around the world is the shortage of qualified teachers. In many countries, particularly in rural areas, there is a shortage of trained teachers, leading to large class sizes and limited resources. In addition, many teachers may lack the necessary training and support to effectively teach in modern classrooms, particularly when it comes to using technology and integrating diverse perspectives.

The quality of education is another challenge that many education systems face. While access to education is important, it is equally important to ensure that students receive a high-quality education that prepares them for success in the workforce and in life. Unfortunately, many education systems around the world struggle with issues such as outdated curricula, inadequate teacher training, and a lack of resources and infrastructure.

In recent years, there has been growing interest in addressing these challenges and improving access to education around the world. Many countries have implemented policies and initiatives to expand access to education, particularly for disadvantaged and marginalized communities. Additionally, there has been a growing focus on improving the quality of education and promoting innovation and creativity in the classroom.

This is where Metawallah comes in. By offering free educational courses in all domains, Metawallah is helping to address the challenges facing education systems around the world. By providing access to high-quality educational resources and training, Metawallah is helping to level the playing field and ensure that all students have the opportunity to learn and succeed. Additionally, by emphasizing innovation, creativity, and critical thinking, Metawallah is helping to prepare students for the challenges and opportunities of the modern world.

In conclusion, education systems vary widely around the world, with each system facing its own set of strengths, weaknesses, and challenges. While some countries offer highly centralized and structured systems, others opt for a more decentralized and flexible approach. Regardless of the approach, all education systems should prioritize access to education and emphasize critical thinking, problem-solving, and creativity. By doing so, we can help to ensure that all students have the opportunity to learn and succeed, regardless of where they live in the world.

CHAPTER FIVE

Challenges faced by students due to financial constraints

Education is one of the most important investments that one can make in their future. Unfortunately, for many students, financial constraints can present significant barriers to achieving their educational goals. In this article, we will explore the challenges faced by students due to financial constraints and how these barriers can be overcome.

One of the most significant challenges faced by students due to financial constraints is a lack of access to resources. Students who come from low-income families often lack access to basic resources such as textbooks, computers, and internet connectivity. This can make it difficult for them to keep up with their studies, complete assignments, and access online learning materials. Students who cannot afford basic resources may also be unable to participate in extracurricular activities or field trips, which can limit their exposure to new experiences and opportunities.

Another major challenge is the cost of tuition and fees. The rising cost of higher education is a growing concern for many students and families, particularly in developed countries such as the United States. High tuition and fees can make it difficult for students to afford college or university, and can force them to take out large student loans. This debt can be a burden for years after graduation, making it difficult to start a career, buy a home, or start a family.

Financial constraints can also impact a student's ability to work and attend school at the same time. Many students need to work to support themselves and pay for their education, but balancing work and school can be difficult. Students who work long hours may find it difficult to keep up with their studies, and may not have time for extracurricular activities or internships that can help them build their skills and prepare for their future careers.

In addition, financial constraints can also have an impact on a student's mental health. The stress of worrying about finances, debt, and the future can take a toll on a student's well-being. Students who cannot afford basic necessities such as food, housing, or healthcare may experience anxiety, depression, or other mental health issues. These challenges can make it even more difficult to succeed academically and achieve their career goals.

Fortunately, there are a number of solutions to help students overcome financial constraints and achieve their educational goals. One of the most effective ways to help students is through financial aid programs, such as grants, scholarships, and student loans. These programs can help cover the cost of tuition, fees, and living expenses, and can make it easier for students to pursue their educational goals without the burden of excessive debt.

In addition, many universities and colleges offer programs and resources to help students who are facing financial constraints. These can include academic support programs, mentorship opportunities, and financial literacy training. Universities and colleges can also help connect students with external resources, such as community organizations, to provide additional support and resources.

Another solution to financial constraints is through online education. Many online education platforms, including Metawallah, offer free or low-cost courses in a wide range of subjects. These courses can help students build their skills and knowledge without the burden of high tuition and fees, and can be completed at their own pace and on their own schedule.

Finally, it is important to remember that financial constraints do not define a student's potential for success. While it can be challenging, it is possible for students to overcome financial barriers and achieve their educational goals. By seeking out resources, support, and solutions to financial constraints, students can take important steps towards building a bright and successful future.

Impact of financial constraints on academic performance: Financial constraints can have a direct impact on a student's academic performance. For example, students who cannot afford to pay for tutoring or academic resources may fall behind in their studies, leading to poor grades and low self-esteem. In addition, financial constraints can force students to take on extra work or reduce their course load, leading to a longer time to graduation and lower academic achievement.

Cultural and social barriers to education: Financial constraints are not the only barriers to education that students face. Students from marginalized communities or underrepresented groups may face additional cultural and social barriers that can make it even more difficult to access educational opportunities. For example, students from low-income backgrounds may not have the same cultural expectations or social support networks that more privileged students have, leading to feelings of isolation and lower levels of academic success.

Impact of financial constraints on mental health: Financial constraints can have a profound impact on a student's mental health. Students who are struggling to make ends meet may feel anxious, depressed, or stressed. In addition, the fear of debt can cause significant stress and anxiety, which can impact a student's overall well-being. Providing mental health support and resources to students who are facing financial constraints is critical to helping them succeed academically.

Student debt and its long-term impact: Student debt is a growing concern for many students and families. In the United States, for example, the total student loan debt has surpassed $1.6 trillion, making it one of the largest sources of consumer debt. Student loan debt can have a significant impact on a student's long-term financial health, making it difficult to buy a home, start a family, or pursue other goals. Finding solutions to reduce the cost of higher education and lower the burden of student debt is critical to improving access to educational opportunities.

International perspectives on financial constraints in education: Financial constraints are not unique to any one country or region. In many developing countries, for example, a lack of access to basic resources such as clean water, electricity, and transportation can make it difficult for students to attend school. In addition, cultural and social norms may limit educational opportunities for certain groups, such as women or those from marginalized communities. Understanding the challenges faced by students in different parts of the world can help inform policies and programs to improve access to education for all.

By exploring the many facets of financial constraints in education, we can begin to identify the root causes of these challenges and work towards finding solutions that will help students overcome them. Whether through financial aid programs, online education, or other innovative approaches, it is possible to help all students access the education they need to succeed in their future endeavors.

In conclusion, financial constraints can present significant challenges for students pursuing their educational goals. However, through a combination of financial aid programs, university and college resources, online education, and personal perseverance, students can overcome these challenges and achieve their academic and career aspirations. Metawallah and other free or low-cost online educational platforms can help provide access to resources that can help students

CHAPTER SIX

Need for free education

Education is an essential tool for personal and societal development. It opens up opportunities for individuals and provides the necessary knowledge and skills to improve their quality of life. However, the cost of education has become increasingly expensive, making it challenging for many individuals to access it. This has resulted in an inequality in access to education and a significant gap between the rich and the poor. The need for free education has become increasingly important to address these disparities and create a level playing field for all individuals.

The Importance of Education

Education is a fundamental human right that should be accessible to everyone, regardless of their socioeconomic status. It equips individuals with the necessary knowledge and skills to succeed in their chosen field and contributes to personal development. Education also plays a vital role in the economic growth of a country, as it leads to increased productivity, innovation, and development. It is also essential for social and cultural development, as it promotes critical thinking, cultural awareness, and tolerance.

Barriers to Education

Despite the importance of education, access to it remains limited for many individuals due to various barriers. One of the significant barriers is the cost of education, which has been on the rise in recent years. The high cost of tuition fees, textbooks, and other education-related expenses has made it challenging for low-income families to afford education. Additionally, the lack of access to basic resources such as transportation and internet connectivity has limited access to education in remote or underdeveloped areas. Social and cultural norms can also serve as barriers to education, especially for women or marginalized groups.

The Need for Free Education

Free education can be the solution to address these barriers and create a level playing field for all individuals. It provides access to quality education without the financial burden that comes with it, thus creating an equal opportunity for all. Free education ensures that everyone has the opportunity to access education, regardless of their financial situation, and promotes equity in access to educational opportunities. It also contributes to the development of a skilled and knowledgeable workforce, which leads to economic growth and development.

The Role of Free Education in Personal and Societal Development

Free education provides the necessary knowledge and skills to individuals to succeed in their chosen fields. It contributes to personal development and improves the quality of life of individuals. Free education also plays a significant role in the development of society. It promotes social and cultural awareness, critical thinking, and tolerance, contributing to the development of a more educated and informed society. Additionally, free education leads to a more skilled and knowledgeable workforce, which leads to economic growth and development.

The Challenges of Implementing Free Education

While the benefits of free education are numerous, there are also challenges associated with its implementation. The most significant challenge is the cost of implementing free education, which can be significant. It requires funding for tuition fees, textbooks, and other education-related expenses, which can be a significant burden on the government's budget. Additionally, there may be resistance from educational institutions and stakeholders who may be resistant to change or concerned about the quality of education provided under a free education system.

Examples of Free Education Programs

Several countries have implemented free education programs to address the barriers to education and provide equal access to education. For example, in Finland, education is free for all students, including foreign students. In Germany, all public universities provide free education to students, regardless of their nationality. In Brazil, the government has implemented the Bolsa Familia program, which provides financial assistance to families with school-aged children, ensuring that they can afford education.

Conclusion

Free education is an essential tool for personal and societal development. It provides access to quality education without the financial burden that comes with it, creating an equal opportunity for all. While there are challenges associated with its implementation, it is essential to address the barriers to education and provide access to education for all individuals

• 25 •

Overview of different types of free education

Education is a fundamental right, and access to quality education is essential for the growth and development of individuals and society as a whole. However, education can be expensive, and not everyone can afford to pay for it. This is where free education comes in. Free education is a form of education that is accessible to all, regardless of their economic status. In this article, we will provide an overview of different types of free education.

Public Schools:

Public schools are schools that are funded and operated by the government. Public schools offer free education to all students, and there are no fees associated with attending them. Public schools are available at the elementary, middle, and high school levels, and they offer a wide range of subjects and extracurricular activities. Public schools are an excellent option for students who cannot afford to attend private schools.

Community Colleges:

Community colleges are two-year colleges that offer associate degrees and vocational training programs. Community colleges are often more affordable than four-year colleges and universities, and they offer a wide range of courses in various fields, including business, healthcare, and technology. Community colleges are an excellent option for students who want to start their education journey but cannot afford to attend a four-year college or university.

MOOCs:

Massive Open Online Courses (MOOCs) are online courses that are available to anyone, anywhere in the world, for free. MOOCs are offered by prestigious universities such as Harvard, MIT, and Stanford, and they cover a wide range of subjects, including computer science, engineering, and business. MOOCs are an excellent option for people who want to learn new skills and advance their careers without paying for traditional education.

Open Educational Resources:

Open Educational Resources (OERs) are educational materials that are available for free online. OERs include textbooks, videos, and lesson plans that have been created by educators and made available for anyone to use. OERs are an excellent option for students who cannot afford to buy expensive textbooks or for educators who want to create customized learning materials for their students.

Apprenticeships:

Apprenticeships are training programs that combine on-the-job training with classroom instruction. Apprenticeships are available in a wide range of fields, including construction, healthcare, and information technology. Apprenticeships are an excellent option for people who want to learn a trade and gain valuable work experience while earning a wage.

Scholarships:

Scholarships are awards that are given to students based on academic merit, financial need, or other criteria. Scholarships can be used to pay for tuition, books, and other education-related expenses. Scholarships are an excellent option for students who have demonstrated academic excellence or who are in financial need.

Work-Study Programs:

Work-Study Programs are programs that allow students to work part-time while attending school. Work-study programs provide students with valuable work experience and a wage that can be used to pay for their education. Work-study programs are an excellent option for students who need to earn money to pay for their education.

Conclusion:

Free education is essential for promoting equal access to education and providing opportunities for people to improve their lives and their communities. Public schools, community colleges, MOOCs, OERs, apprenticeships, scholarships, and work-study programs are all excellent options for people who cannot afford traditional education or who want to learn new skills without paying for a traditional education. By taking advantage of these different types of free education, individuals can acquire the knowledge and skills they need to succeed in their careers and in life.

CHAPTER EIGHT

Advantages and disadvantages of each type

Education is essential for personal and societal growth, and access to quality education is critical for everyone. However, education can be expensive, and not everyone can afford it. Free education has become a popular alternative for many people, offering various options to learn without paying for it. In this article, we will provide an overview of the advantages and disadvantages of each type of free education.

Public Schools:

Advantages:

a) Free education: Public schools offer free education to all students. There are no fees associated with attending public schools, which makes them an excellent option for families who cannot afford private schools.

b) Accessible: Public schools are available in almost every community, making them accessible to most students. The government funds public schools, and they have a duty to provide education to everyone.

c) Diversity: Public schools often have a diverse student population, which provides opportunities for students to learn about different cultures and perspectives.

Disadvantages:

a) Limited Curriculum: Public schools often have limited resources, which may restrict the number of courses or extracurricular activities available.

b) Overcrowding: Public schools often have large class sizes, which can make it difficult for students to receive individualized attention from their teachers.

c) Lower quality of education: Public schools are often underfunded, which may lead to lower quality of education compared to private schools.

Community Colleges:

Advantages:

a) Affordable: Community colleges are often more affordable than four-year colleges and universities, making them a great option for students who cannot afford higher education.

b) Vocational training: Community colleges offer vocational training programs that prepare students for a specific career. This means that students can enter the workforce sooner and with the skills they need.

c) Transferability: Community college credits can often be transferred to a four-year college or university, which allows students to start their education journey at a lower cost.

Disadvantages:

a) Limited options: Community colleges offer a limited number of courses and degree programs, which may not suit everyone's needs.

b) Lower quality of education: Community colleges may have a lower quality of education compared to four-year colleges and universities.

c) Less prestigious: Community colleges are often seen as less prestigious than four-year colleges and universities, which may affect job prospects for graduates.

MOOCs:

Advantages:

a) Flexibility: MOOCs can be taken from anywhere in the world, at any time. This makes them a great option for people who have other commitments, such as work or family.

b) Variety: MOOCs offer a wide variety of courses and subjects, which means that there is something for everyone.

c) High-quality education: MOOCs are often taught by professors from prestigious universities, which means that students receive a high-quality education.

Disadvantages:

a) Limited interaction: MOOCs often have limited interaction between students and professors, which can make it difficult for students to receive individualized attention.

b) Lack of motivation: Because MOOCs are often self-paced, students may lack motivation and fall behind.

c) Cost: While MOOCs are generally free, some courses require payment to receive a certificate of completion.

Open Educational Resources:

Advantages:

a) Free: OERs are free to access and use, which makes them an excellent option for students who cannot afford expensive textbooks or other learning materials.

b) Customizable: OERs can be customized to suit individual needs and preferences. This means that educators can create materials that meet the needs of their students.

c) Easy to access: OERs are available online, which means that they can be accessed from anywhere in the world.

CHAPTER NINE

Most popular and respected institutions offering free education

Education is a fundamental human right, and access to quality education should not be limited by one's financial status. While most reputable institutions charge tuition fees, there are some institutions that offer free education to students. In this article, we will provide an overview of the most popular and respected institutions offering free education.

Massachusetts Institute of Technology (MIT):

MIT is a private research university located in Cambridge, Massachusetts, and is considered one of the most prestigious universities in the world. MIT has been offering free online courses since 2002 through its OpenCourseWare (OCW) program. The program provides access to more than 2,400 courses, which include lecture notes, assignments, and exams. MIT OCW covers a wide range of subjects, including computer science, engineering, mathematics, and humanities.

The program is free to access and does not require registration. However, students do not receive course credit or a certificate of completion. The courses are designed for self-paced learning, and students can access the materials at any time.

Harvard University:

Harvard University is a private research university located in Cambridge, Massachusetts. Harvard is widely regarded as one of the most prestigious universities in the world and is known for its excellence in research and education. Harvard has been offering free online courses since 2012 through its HarvardX program. The program provides access to more than 100 courses, which include lecture videos, assignments, and exams.

The program is free to access, and students can earn a certificate of completion for a fee. The courses cover a wide range of subjects, including computer science, humanities, business, and law.

Stanford University:

Stanford University is a private research university located in Stanford, California. Stanford is known for its excellence in research and education and is considered one of the most prestigious universities in the world. Stanford has been offering free online courses since 2011 through its Stanford Online program. The program provides access to more than 200 courses, which include lecture videos, assignments, and exams.

The program is free to access, and students can earn a certificate of completion for a fee. The courses cover a wide range of subjects, including computer science, engineering, humanities, and social sciences.

Yale University:

Yale University is a private research university located in New Haven, Connecticut. Yale is known for its excellence in research and education and is considered one of the most prestigious universities in the world. Yale has been offering free online courses since 2007 through its Open Yale Courses program. The program provides access to more than 40 courses, which include lecture videos, transcripts, and reading lists.

The program is free to access, and students do not receive course credit or a certificate of completion. The courses cover a wide range of subjects, including humanities, social sciences, and science.

Khan Academy:

Khan Academy is a non-profit organization that provides free online education to students of all ages. The organization was founded in 2008 by Salman Khan, and it offers more than 5,000 educational videos on a wide range of subjects, including math, science, history, and economics. The videos are self-paced, and students can access them at any time.

Khan Academy also offers interactive exercises and quizzes that allow students to practice what they have learned. The exercises are designed to adapt to the student's level of understanding and provide instant feedback. Khan Academy has partnerships with schools and universities around the world, and its content is translated into more than 36 languages.

Coursera:

Coursera is an online learning platform that offers free and paid courses from some of the world's leading universities and institutions.

CHAPTER TEN

Different online platforms that offer free courses and resources

In today's digital age, online learning has become an increasingly popular way for people to expand their knowledge and skills. With the rise of free online courses, anyone with an internet connection can now access high-quality educational resources from the comfort of their own home. In this article, we will take a look at some of the best online platforms that offer free courses and resources, covering a wide range of topics and subjects.

Coursera

Coursera is one of the most popular online learning platforms in the world. The platform offers free online courses from some of the best universities and institutions in the world. The courses cover a wide range of topics, from business and technology to health and wellness. Each course is taught by industry experts, and students can earn certificates upon completion of the course.

edX

edX is another popular online learning platform that offers free courses from top universities such as Harvard, MIT, and Berkeley. The platform offers a wide range of courses, including computer science, business, engineering, and humanities. edX also offers certificates for its courses, which can be a great addition to a resume or portfolio.

Udemy

Udemy is an online learning platform that offers both free and paid courses. The platform has a vast library of courses covering a wide range of subjects, including business, technology, and personal development. While not all courses are free, Udemy regularly offers discounts and promotions, allowing students to access courses at a reduced cost.

Khan Academy

Khan Academy is a non-profit organization that provides free educational resources to students around the world. The platform offers courses in math, science, economics, and computer programming, among others. Khan Academy also provides resources for teachers, allowing them to incorporate the platform's resources into their lesson plans.

Codecademy

Codecademy is an online learning platform that focuses specifically on teaching coding and programming. The platform offers free courses in languages such as HTML, CSS, and JavaScript, as well as more advanced courses in Python, Ruby, and SQL. Codecademy also offers a paid subscription service, which provides access to additional courses and features.

FutureLearn

FutureLearn is an online learning platform that offers free courses from universities and institutions around the world. The platform covers a wide range of topics, including business, healthcare, and social sciences. FutureLearn also offers paid courses and degrees, allowing students to earn formal qualifications.

Alison

Alison is a free online learning platform that offers courses in a wide range of subjects, including business, technology, and health. The platform provides courses from leading experts in their respective fields, and students can earn certificates upon completion of the course.

OpenLearn

OpenLearn is a free online learning platform provided by The Open University. The platform offers courses in a wide range of subjects, including arts and humanities, business and management, and science and technology. OpenLearn also provides free resources, such as articles and videos, allowing students to supplement their learning.

MIT OpenCourseWare

MIT OpenCourseWare is an initiative by the Massachusetts Institute of Technology (MIT) that provides free educational resources to the public. The platform offers course materials for hundreds of courses, covering subjects such as engineering, computer science, and economics. While the courses do not offer formal certification, the platform provides an excellent opportunity for self-directed learning.

Harvard Online Learning

Harvard Online Learning is an online learning platform that offers free courses and resources from Harvard University. The platform covers a wide range of subjects, including business, law, and healthcare. While the courses do not provide formal certification, students can earn a certificate of completion for certain courses.

CHAPTER ELEVEN

Most popular and respected platforms for online learning

The digital age has brought about a paradigm shift in the way people learn. With the rise of online learning platforms, students now have access to a wealth of educational resources from some of the world's top universities and institutions. These platforms offer a range of courses and certifications that are recognized by employers and industry professionals. In this article, we will take a look at some of the most popular and respected platforms for online learning.

Coursera

Coursera is a popular online learning platform that offers courses from top universities and institutions around the world. The platform provides over 4,000 courses in a variety of fields, including business, technology, and social sciences. Coursera partners with over 200 universities, including Stanford, Yale, and Duke. Each course is taught by experts in their respective fields, and students can earn certificates upon completion of the course. Coursera also offers specialization programs, which provide a deeper understanding of a specific subject area.

edX

edX is another popular online learning platform that offers courses from some of the best universities in the world, including Harvard, MIT, and Berkeley. The platform provides over 3,000 courses in a variety of fields, including computer science, engineering, and humanities. edX also offers MicroMasters programs, which provide a deeper understanding of a specific subject area and can be used to earn credit towards a full Master's degree. Students can earn certificates of completion for the courses they take on edX.

Udacity

Udacity is an online learning platform that focuses on technology and programming courses. The platform partners with industry leaders, such as Google, Amazon, and Facebook, to create courses that are relevant to current industry trends. Udacity offers courses in a variety of fields, including artificial intelligence, data science, and web development. The platform provides project-based learning, which allows students to apply their skills in real-world scenarios. Udacity also offers Nanodegree programs, which provide a deeper understanding of a specific subject area and can be used to enhance a student's resume.

Khan Academy

Khan Academy is a non-profit organization that provides free educational resources to students around the world. The platform offers courses in a variety of fields, including math, science, and humanities. Khan Academy provides resources for teachers, allowing them to incorporate the platform's resources into their lesson plans. The platform also provides personalized learning, which allows students to learn at their own pace.

Codecademy

Codecademy is an online learning platform that focuses specifically on coding and programming. The platform offers courses in languages such as HTML, CSS, and JavaScript, as well as more advanced courses in Python, Ruby, and SQL. Codecademy provides project-based learning, which allows students to apply their skills in real-world scenarios. The platform also offers a Pro version, which provides access to additional features and courses.

FutureLearn

FutureLearn is an online learning platform that offers courses from leading universities and institutions around the world. The platform provides courses in a variety of fields, including business, healthcare, and social sciences. FutureLearn also offers paid courses and degrees, allowing students to earn formal qualifications. The platform provides discussion forums, which allow students to interact with each other and the instructors.

Alison

Alison is a free online learning platform that offers courses in a variety of fields, including business, technology, and health. The platform provides courses from leading experts in their respective fields, and students can earn certificates upon completion of the course. Alison also offers a premium version, which provides access to additional courses and features.

LinkedIn Learning

LinkedIn Learning is an online learning platform that provides courses in a variety of fields, including business, technology, and creative skills.

CHAPTER TWELVE

Tips on how to find the best online courses

Online learning has gained significant popularity over the years, with many people taking advantage of the convenience and flexibility that it offers. However, not all online courses are created equal, and it's crucial to find the best online courses that align with your goals and interests. In this article, we will provide tips on how to find the best online courses that will help you achieve your learning objectives.

Define your goals

Before embarking on a search for online courses, it's essential to define your goals. What do you want to achieve by taking an online course? Are you looking to enhance your skills, start a new career, or pursue personal interests? By having a clear understanding of your goals, you can narrow down your search and focus on courses that align with your objectives.

Look for accredited courses

When searching for online courses, it's crucial to ensure that the courses are accredited. Accreditation is an essential aspect of any educational institution or course, as it demonstrates that the course meets specific standards of quality and rigor. Accreditation also ensures that the course credits can be transferred to other institutions, and the certification is recognized by employers.

Check the course curriculum

Before enrolling in an online course, it's essential to review the course curriculum to ensure that it aligns with your goals and interests. Check the course syllabus and read the course description to get an idea of what the course covers. Look for courses that provide a comprehensive and practical approach to learning, with assignments and projects that allow you to apply your knowledge in real-world scenarios.

Read reviews and ratings

One of the best ways to determine the quality of an online course is to read reviews and ratings from previous students. Many online learning platforms have reviews and ratings from past students, which can provide valuable insights into the course's quality, difficulty, and instructor effectiveness. Reviews can also help you determine if the course is suitable for your skill level and learning style.

Check the instructor's qualifications

The instructor is a critical aspect of any online course, and it's essential to ensure that the instructor has the necessary qualifications and expertise in the course subject. Look for instructors who have experience in the field and hold relevant certifications or degrees. You can also research the instructor's background and check if they have published any articles or books related to the course subject.

Consider the format and delivery

Online courses come in various formats and delivery methods, such as pre-recorded lectures, live classes, and interactive learning. It's essential to consider the format and delivery method that works best for your learning style and schedule. For instance, if you prefer a structured learning experience, you may opt for live classes that allow for interaction with the instructor and other students. On the other hand, if you have a busy schedule, pre-recorded lectures may be more convenient.

Evaluate the cost and value

Online courses vary in cost, and it's essential to evaluate the cost and value of the course before enrolling. Consider the course's overall value, including the quality of instruction, the course materials, and the certification or degree. Look for courses that provide a good return on investment and align with your budget.

Take advantage of free trials

Many online learning platforms offer free trials or samples of their courses, which can be an excellent way to determine if the course is suitable for your needs. Take advantage of free trials to get a feel for the course's format, delivery, and content. This can help you determine if the course aligns with your learning objectives and preferences.

Consider the reputation of the platform

When selecting an online course, it's essential to consider the reputation of the learning platform. Look for platforms that have a solid reputation for providing high-quality courses and have partnerships with reputable institutions.

CHAPTER THIRTEEN

Importance of libraries in accessing free education

Libraries are one of the most critical resources available for accessing free education. They are institutions that offer free access to a vast array of information, knowledge, and educational materials, making them indispensable tools in the pursuit of knowledge. Libraries play a crucial role in educating the masses, promoting literacy, and providing equal opportunities for all, regardless of their socio-economic status. In this article, we will discuss the importance of libraries in accessing free education and how they contribute to the development of individuals and society as a whole.

Promoting Literacy

One of the primary functions of libraries is to promote literacy. They provide a wide range of reading materials, including books, newspapers, journals, and magazines, that are essential in developing reading skills. Moreover, libraries offer various programs and services that help children, adolescents, and adults to learn how to read and write. These programs include reading clubs, writing workshops, and literacy classes. Libraries are particularly critical in communities with a high illiteracy rate, as they provide an opportunity for individuals to develop their reading skills and improve their quality of life.

Equal Access to Knowledge

Libraries provide equal access to knowledge, regardless of an individual's socio-economic status. They are open to all, and anyone can access the information they need to further their education. Libraries are especially critical for people who cannot afford to purchase educational materials, such as books or journals, or access the internet. By offering free access to a vast array of educational resources, libraries play a significant role in reducing the gap between the rich and the poor, providing opportunities for all to develop their skills and knowledge.

Supporting Lifelong Learning

Libraries support lifelong learning, a process that involves acquiring new knowledge, skills, and attitudes throughout one's life. They provide a wide range of educational resources, including books, journals, and online resources, that support the educational needs of individuals from early childhood to adulthood. Libraries offer educational programs and services that help people of all ages to acquire new skills and knowledge, such as computer literacy, language learning, and job readiness. They also provide access to educational materials that support personal growth, including self-help books and resources on mental health and wellbeing.

Fostering a Love of Learning

Libraries play an essential role in fostering a love of learning. They offer a welcoming and safe environment for individuals to explore new ideas and learn about a variety of topics. By providing access to educational materials and resources, libraries encourage curiosity, creativity, and critical thinking, fostering a passion for lifelong learning. Moreover, libraries often offer programs and activities that promote learning and engagement, such as book clubs, author talks, and lectures. These programs provide an opportunity for individuals to interact with others who share their interests, promoting a sense of community and connection.

Promoting Research and Innovation

Libraries are critical for promoting research and innovation. They offer a wealth of information and resources that support research in a variety of fields, including science, technology, engineering, and mathematics (STEM), humanities, and social sciences. Libraries often offer specialized resources, such as scientific journals, databases, and archives, that support research in specific fields. Moreover, libraries provide access to technology, such as computers and internet connectivity, that supports research and innovation. By providing access to these resources, libraries play a significant role in advancing knowledge, promoting innovation, and supporting the development of new ideas.

Conclusion

In conclusion, libraries are essential in accessing free education. They play a critical role in promoting literacy, providing equal access to knowledge, supporting lifelong learning, fostering a love of learning, and promoting research and innovation. Libraries offer a wealth of educational resources, including books, journals, magazines, and online resources, that support the educational needs of individuals from early childhood to adulthood. Moreover, libraries provide access to technology, educational programs, and services that

Community resources for learning, such as workshops, seminars, and community centers

Community resources for learning are an essential aspect of education, especially for individuals who may not have access to traditional learning environments. Workshops, seminars, and community centers are just some of the many resources that can provide access to educational opportunities for individuals of all ages and backgrounds. In this article, we will explore the importance of community resources for learning, the types of resources available, and the benefits they offer.

Importance of Community Resources for Learning

Community resources for learning are critical for individuals who may not have access to traditional learning environments, such as schools and universities. For example, workshops and seminars can provide individuals with the opportunity to learn new skills, develop existing skills, and connect with others who share similar interests.

Community centers can also provide access to resources, including technology and educational materials, that may not be available in other settings.

Moreover, community resources for learning can be particularly beneficial for individuals who are looking to change careers or transition into a new field. Workshops and seminars can provide these individuals with the opportunity to learn new skills and gain practical experience, making them more competitive in the job market. Community centers can also offer job training programs, such as computer skills and resume writing, that can be invaluable for individuals who are seeking new employment opportunities.

Types of Community Resources for Learning

There are many types of community resources for learning, each offering unique benefits to individuals seeking educational opportunities. Some of the most common types of resources include:

Workshops and Seminars

Workshops and seminars are short-term educational programs that offer individuals the opportunity to learn new skills or develop existing ones. These programs can range in length from a few hours to several days and can cover a wide range of topics, from personal development to professional training. Workshops and seminars are often led by experts in the field and may include hands-on training or interactive activities.

Community Centers

Community centers are facilities that provide access to resources and services that promote community engagement and education. These centers can offer a wide range of programs and services, including job training, education and literacy programs, health and wellness classes, and after-school programs for children. Community centers can also provide access to technology, such as computers and internet connectivity, that can be essential for learning and professional development.

Public Libraries

Public libraries are community resources that offer access to a vast array of educational materials, including books, journals, and online resources. Libraries can also provide educational programs and services, including reading clubs, writing workshops, and computer skills training. Public libraries are often free and open to all, making them an excellent resource for individuals who may not have access to educational materials or resources.

Online Learning Platforms

Online learning platforms, such as Coursera and edX, offer individuals the opportunity to learn new skills and gain knowledge from the comfort of their own home. These platforms offer courses from top universities and institutions around the world, covering a wide range of topics, including business, technology, and the arts. Online learning platforms can be an excellent resource for individuals who may not have access to traditional learning environments or who are looking to learn at their own pace.

Benefits of Community Resources for Learning

Community resources for learning offer many benefits to individuals seeking educational opportunities. These benefits include:

Increased Access to Educational Opportunities

Community resources for learning can provide individuals with access to educational opportunities that may not be available in other settings. For example, workshops and seminars can offer practical training and hands-on experience, while community centers can provide access to resources, such as technology and educational materials, that may be essential for learning.

Professional Development

Community resources for learning can also offer individuals the opportunity to develop new skills or gain knowledge that can be invaluable in their professional lives.

CHAPTER FIFTEEN

How to find free resources in your community

Access to education is essential for personal growth, professional development, and economic prosperity. Unfortunately, the cost of education can be a significant barrier for many individuals. However, there are many free resources in communities that can help individuals access the education they need. In this article, we will explore how to find free resources in your community for education, including where to look, what to look for, and how to make the most of these resources.

Public Libraries

Public libraries are a valuable resource for education and learning. They provide access to a vast collection of books, journals, magazines, and online resources, all of which are available for free. Libraries also offer various educational programs and services, including book clubs, writing workshops, and computer classes.

To find a public library in your community, check the local phone book, or search online. Many libraries have websites where you can search for books, request items, and access online resources.

Community Centers

Community centers are another excellent resource for education and learning. They offer a wide range of programs and services, including after-school programs, tutoring, job training, and computer classes. Community centers can also be a hub for community events, such as workshops and seminars.

To find a community center in your area, check with your local government, or search online. Many community centers have websites where you can find information about programs, events, and services.

Non-Profit Organizations

Non-profit organizations are a valuable resource for education and learning. Many non-profits offer educational programs and services, such as tutoring, mentoring, and job training. Some non-profits also provide financial assistance for education, such as scholarships and grants.

To find non-profit organizations in your area, check with your local government, or search online. Many non-profits have websites where you can find information about programs and services.

Local Colleges and Universities

Local colleges and universities are another valuable resource for education and learning. Many colleges and universities offer free courses and workshops, as well as access to educational materials and resources. These institutions may also offer financial assistance for education, such as scholarships and grants.

To find local colleges and universities in your area, check with your local government, or search online. Many colleges and universities have websites where you can find information about courses, programs, and financial assistance.

Online Learning Platforms

Online learning platforms, such as Coursera and edX, offer a wide range of courses and programs that are available for free. These platforms provide access to courses from top universities and institutions around the world, covering a wide range of topics, including business, technology, and the arts.

To find online learning platforms, search online or check with your local library or community center. Many libraries and community centers offer access to online learning platforms as part of their services.

Tips for Making the Most of Free Resources in Your Community

Research the resources available in your community and take advantage of as many as possible.

Attend workshops, seminars, and other events to learn new skills and gain knowledge.

Network with other individuals in your community who are also taking advantage of free resources for education.

Keep a record of your progress, including the courses you have taken and the skills you have learned.

Take advantage of financial assistance programs, such as scholarships and grants, to further your education.

Conclusion

Free resources for education are available in many communities, providing individuals with access to the knowledge and skills they need to succeed. Whether you are looking to further your education, gain new skills, or transition into a new career, there are many resources available to help you achieve your goals. By taking advantage of these resources, you can improve your life, your career, and your future.

Step-by-step guide to creating a self-learning plan

Learning is a lifelong process, and it's essential to have a self-learning plan to achieve your goals. A self-learning plan can help you to improve your skills, knowledge, and abilities. It can also help you to achieve personal and professional development. In this article, we will provide a step-by-step guide to creating a self-learning plan.

Step 1: Identify Your Goals

The first step in creating a self-learning plan is to identify your goals. What do you want to achieve? Do you want to improve your job performance, learn a new skill, or pursue a new career? It's important to be specific about your goals and to make them achievable. Once you have identified your goals, you can create a plan to achieve them.

Step 2: Determine Your Learning Style

The next step in creating a self-learning plan is to determine your learning style. Everyone has a different learning style, and it's important to understand your own. There are four main learning styles: visual, auditory, kinesthetic, and read/write. Visual learners prefer to see information, auditory learners prefer to hear information, kinesthetic learners prefer to learn through movement, and read/write learners prefer to learn through reading and writing. Once you have determined your learning style, you can choose learning methods that suit your style.

Step 3: Choose Learning Methods

The third step in creating a self-learning plan is to choose learning methods. There are various learning methods, including online courses, books, seminars, workshops, and mentorship. Choose methods that suit your learning style and align with your goals. Online courses are an excellent option for people who prefer to learn at their own pace. Books are a great option for people who prefer to read and learn independently. Seminars and workshops are ideal for people who prefer to learn in a group setting. Mentorship is an excellent option for people who want to learn from someone who has experience in their chosen field.

Step 4: Create a Schedule

The next step in creating a self-learning plan is to create a schedule. It's essential to allocate time for learning and to stick to a schedule. Determine how much time you can commit to learning each day or week and schedule your learning activities accordingly. Be realistic about your schedule and ensure that you have enough time to complete each activity. If you find that you're struggling to stick to your schedule, try breaking it down into smaller tasks.

Step 5: Set Milestones

The fifth step in creating a self-learning plan is to set milestones. Milestones are specific goals that you want to achieve along the way. Setting milestones can help you to stay motivated and focused. Determine what you want to achieve and set a deadline for achieving each milestone. For example, if your goal is to learn a new language, your milestones could be to learn 50 new words by the end of the month, to have a basic conversation in the language by the end of the quarter, and to be able to write a paragraph in the language by the end of the year.

Step 6: Measure Your Progress

The sixth step in creating a self-learning plan is to measure your progress. It's important to track your progress and to see how far you've come. Determine how you will measure your progress, such as by taking quizzes, writing essays, or completing assignments. Regularly check your progress against your milestones to ensure that you're on track.

Step 7: Adjust Your Plan

The final step in creating a self-learning plan is to adjust your plan. Your plan should be flexible, and you should be willing to adjust it as necessary. If you find that you're struggling with a particular learning method, try a different method.

CHAPTER SEVENTEEN

Importance of setting goals and developing a schedule

Setting goals and developing a schedule are two essential steps in achieving success in any area of life. Whether it's personal or professional, having goals and a schedule can help individuals to stay motivated, focused, and organized. In this article, we will explore the importance of setting goals and developing a schedule and how these two elements can help individuals to achieve their desired outcomes.

The Importance of Setting Goals

Setting goals is the first step in achieving success. Goals provide individuals with a clear direction, purpose, and focus. Without goals, individuals may find themselves lost, lacking motivation, and unsure of what to do next. Setting goals allows individuals to focus on what is important, and what they want to achieve.

Goals also help individuals to measure their progress. When individuals have a clear goal in mind, they can break it down into smaller, achievable steps. This allows individuals to see their progress and determine whether they are on track to achieve their goal.

Setting goals also provides individuals with a sense of accomplishment. When individuals achieve their goals, they feel a sense of pride and satisfaction, which can boost their self-esteem and confidence. Goals provide individuals with a sense of purpose and a reason to keep pushing forward.

The Importance of Developing a Schedule

Developing a schedule is another essential step in achieving success. A schedule provides individuals with a framework for their day or week, allowing them to organize their time and priorities. A schedule helps individuals to stay focused and motivated, ensuring that they are using their time wisely and effectively.

A schedule also helps individuals to avoid procrastination. When individuals have a clear plan for their day, they are less likely to waste time or become distracted. A schedule provides individuals with a sense of urgency and accountability, ensuring that they are working towards their goals.

A schedule also helps individuals to manage their time effectively. With a schedule in place, individuals can allocate their time for work, leisure, and other activities. This allows individuals to balance their personal and professional life and to ensure that they are not neglecting any important areas of their life.

Developing a schedule also helps individuals to build habits. When individuals stick to a schedule, they are building a routine and establishing habits. This makes it easier for individuals to stay focused, motivated, and on track with their goals.

How to Set Goals

Setting goals may seem like a simple task, but it's important to do it correctly to ensure success. Here are some steps to follow when setting goals:

Identify your goal: Determine what you want to achieve and why it's important to you.

Make it specific: Make sure your goal is specific and measurable. This will help you to track your progress and determine when you have achieved your goal.

Break it down: Break your goal down into smaller, achievable steps. This will make it easier to work towards your goal and track your progress.

Make it realistic: Make sure your goal is achievable and realistic. Setting unrealistic goals can lead to disappointment and frustration.

Set a deadline: Set a deadline for achieving your goal. This will provide you with a sense of urgency and accountability.

How to Develop a Schedule

Developing a schedule is a crucial step in achieving success. Here are some steps to follow when developing a schedule:

Determine your priorities: Determine what's important to you and what you want to achieve.

Allocate time: Allocate time for each activity, ensuring that you have enough time to complete each task.

Be realistic: Be realistic about your schedule and ensure that you have enough time to complete each task. Don't overcommit yourself, as this can lead to burnout and frustration.

Make it flexible: Make your schedule flexible, allowing for unexpected events or changes in your priorities.

Stick to it: Stick to your schedule

CHAPTER EIGHTEEN

Tips on how to stay motivated and track progress

Motivation is the driving force behind any successful endeavor. Whether you are trying to reach a personal or professional goal, staying motivated is essential. However, it can be challenging to maintain motivation over an extended period. It's easy to get bogged down by setbacks, obstacles, and distractions, and lose sight of your progress. This is where tracking your progress comes into play. By keeping track of your progress, you can see how far you have come and stay motivated to continue. In this article, we will explore tips on how to stay motivated and track progress towards achieving your goals.

Tip #1: Set Specific and Realistic Goals

The first step in staying motivated is to set specific and realistic goals. Your goals should be clear and well-defined, with specific metrics for success. This allows you to measure your progress, which is essential for staying motivated. Goals should also be realistic, taking into account your resources, time, and capabilities. Setting unrealistic goals can lead to frustration and loss of motivation, so it's important to be honest with yourself about what you can achieve.

Tip #2: Break Down Your Goals into Smaller Tasks

Breaking down your goals into smaller tasks is an effective way to stay motivated. When goals are too big or vague, it can be challenging to make progress. By breaking down your goals into smaller, more manageable tasks, you can work towards achieving them one step at a time. This approach helps to prevent overwhelm and keeps you motivated by allowing you to see progress with each completed task.

Tip #3: Create a Schedule and Stick to It

Creating a schedule is an essential step in staying motivated. A schedule helps you to organize your time and priorities, allowing you to work towards your goals in a structured and efficient manner. When creating your schedule, make sure to allocate enough time for each task and include breaks to avoid burnout. Once you have created your schedule, it's important to stick to it to develop a routine and establish good habits.

Tip #4: Celebrate Your Achievements

Celebrating your achievements is a powerful motivator. When you achieve a goal or complete a task, take the time to acknowledge and celebrate your accomplishment. This could be as simple as treating yourself to a favorite meal or taking a day off to relax. Celebrating your achievements helps to boost your confidence and motivation, making it easier to stay focused on your goals.

Tip #5: Find an Accountability Partner

Having an accountability partner is another effective way to stay motivated. An accountability partner can be a friend, family member, or colleague who holds you responsible for your progress. By checking in with your accountability partner regularly, you are more likely to stay on track and motivated. An accountability partner can also provide support, encouragement, and feedback when you need it.

Tip #6: Use Visual Aids to Track Progress

Visual aids are a helpful tool for tracking progress and staying motivated. This could be a chart, graph, or a list of tasks with checkboxes. Visual aids provide a tangible representation of your progress, making it easier to see how far you have come and how much further you need to go. As you complete tasks or reach milestones, you can mark them off on your visual aid, providing a sense of accomplishment and motivation to continue.

Tip #7: Practice Positive Self-Talk

Positive self-talk is a powerful motivator. The way you talk to yourself can have a significant impact on your motivation and confidence. By practicing positive self-talk, you can replace negative self-talk with positive affirmations, boosting your self-esteem and motivation. For example, instead of saying, "I can't do this," try saying, "I can do this, and I will succeed."

CHAPTER NINETEEN

Skills that are in demand in the current job market

The job market is constantly evolving, and the skills that are in demand today may not be the same as those in demand tomorrow. In recent years, advancements in technology have brought about significant changes in the job market, with some traditional roles being phased out and new roles emerging. This means that job seekers need to stay abreast of the skills that are currently in demand in order to remain competitive. In this article, we will explore the skills that are in demand in the current job market and how you can acquire them.

Digital Literacy and Technology Skills

One of the most significant changes in the job market in recent years is the growing demand for digital literacy and technology skills. As businesses become more reliant on technology, job seekers need to have a strong foundation in digital literacy and the ability to use different software applications. Some of the in-demand technology skills include proficiency in programming languages like Python and Java, knowledge of cloud computing, cybersecurity, and artificial intelligence. These skills are particularly important for roles in software development, data analytics, cybersecurity, and digital marketing.

Creativity and Innovation

Innovation is a driving force behind growth and success in the current job market. Employers are increasingly seeking candidates who can think outside the box and come up with creative solutions to problems. This means that individuals with skills in creativity and innovation are in high demand across different industries. Creative skills include graphic design, user experience design, content creation, and copywriting, while innovation skills include ideation, problem-solving, and product development.

Soft Skills

Soft skills are personal attributes that enable individuals to interact effectively with others. These skills are increasingly in demand in the job market, with employers recognizing their importance in fostering collaboration, communication, and teamwork. Some of the most in-demand soft skills include leadership, communication, adaptability, emotional intelligence, and time management. These skills are particularly important for roles in management, customer service, and human resources.

Data Analysis and Interpretation

Data is a valuable resource in the current job market, with businesses using it to drive decision-making and improve performance. As such, individuals with skills in data analysis and interpretation are in high demand. These skills include proficiency in data analytics software like Tableau and SQL, as well as the ability to manipulate and analyze large data sets. Data analysis and interpretation skills are particularly important for roles in finance, marketing, and operations.

Customer Service and Sales Skills

Customer service and sales skills are always in demand in the job market, with businesses recognizing the importance of providing excellent customer experiences. Individuals with skills in customer service and sales are able to engage with customers, build relationships, and drive sales. These skills include active listening, problem-solving, persuasion, and customer empathy. Customer service and sales skills are particularly important for roles in sales, marketing, and customer service.

Multilingualism and Cultural Awareness

Globalization has led to an increase in demand for individuals with multilingualism and cultural awareness skills. These skills are particularly important for businesses that operate across different regions and countries. Multilingualism skills include the ability to speak and write in multiple languages, while cultural awareness skills include knowledge of different cultures and customs. These skills are particularly important for roles in international business, diplomacy, and translation.

Conclusion

In conclusion, the job market is constantly evolving, and job seekers need to stay abreast of the skills that are currently in demand. In the current job market, digital literacy and technology skills, creativity and innovation, soft skills, data analysis and interpretation, customer service and sales skills, and multilingualism and cultural awareness are in high demand. Acquiring these skills can help job seekers remain competitive and increase their chances of landing their desired roles. Whether you are a recent graduate or an experienced professional, it's important to invest

CHAPTER TWENTY

Tips on how to acquire these skills for free

Education is one of the most important tools for personal growth and professional success. However, the cost of acquiring skills and knowledge can be a significant barrier for many individuals. Fortunately, there are many ways to acquire skills for free. In this article, we will discuss some tips on how to acquire skills for free in education.

Use Open Educational Resources (OER)

Open Educational Resources (OER) are free educational materials that can be used for teaching and learning. These resources include textbooks, videos, and other learning materials that are available for free on the internet. OER can be found on websites such as OpenStax, Khan Academy, and Coursera. By using these resources, you can gain knowledge and skills without having to pay for expensive textbooks and courses.

Take advantage of MOOCs

Massive Open Online Courses (MOOCs) are online courses that are available for free. MOOCs are offered by universities and other organizations, and they cover a wide range of topics, from computer science to psychology. By taking MOOCs, you can acquire knowledge and skills that are relevant to your personal and professional goals. Some popular MOOC platforms include Coursera, edX, and Udemy.

Attend webinars and workshops

Many organizations and institutions offer free webinars and workshops on various topics. By attending these events, you can gain knowledge and skills from experts in the field. These events are usually hosted online, which makes them easily accessible to anyone with an internet connection. You can find free webinars and workshops by searching online for events in your area of interest.

Participate in online communities

Online communities are a great way to connect with others who share your interests and goals. By participating in online communities, you can learn from others and share your own knowledge and experience. Some popular online communities include Reddit, Quora, and Stack Overflow. These communities are free to join and offer a wealth of knowledge and resources.

Volunteer or intern

Volunteering and interning are great ways to gain hands-on experience and skills. Many organizations offer volunteer and internship opportunities that allow you to gain practical skills and knowledge in your area of interest. Volunteering and interning are also great ways to build your resume and network with professionals in your field.

In conclusion, there are many ways to acquire skills for free in education. By using open educational resources, taking advantage of MOOCs, attending webinars and workshops, participating in online communities, and volunteering or interning, you can gain the knowledge and skills you need to succeed in your personal and professional life. With these tips, you can acquire the skills you need without breaking the bank.

Benefits of acquiring new skills

Acquiring new skills is essential for personal growth and professional development. Whether you're an entry-level employee or a seasoned professional, continuously learning new skills can help you stay relevant, competitive, and adaptable in a rapidly changing job market. In this article, we will discuss the benefits of acquiring new skills, including improved job prospects, increased earning potential, personal growth, and better job satisfaction.

Improved job prospects

One of the most significant benefits of acquiring new skills is improved job prospects. By learning new skills, you become more valuable to your current employer and more attractive to potential employers. This is especially true in industries that are rapidly changing, such as technology or healthcare. In these industries, employers are looking for employees who have the latest knowledge and skills, and are willing to invest in their employees' professional development.

Furthermore, having a diverse range of skills can help you stand out in a crowded job market. Employers are looking for candidates who have a broad range of skills and can bring a unique perspective to the job. By acquiring new skills, you can differentiate yourself from other job candidates and increase your chances of landing your dream job.

Increased earning potential

Acquiring new skills can also lead to increased earning potential. Employees who have a diverse range of skills and knowledge are often more highly valued by employers, and may be offered higher salaries or promotions. Additionally, having a broader range of skills can make you eligible for a wider range of jobs and industries, which may offer higher salaries.

For example, if you work in a sales role but also have expertise in digital marketing, you may be eligible for higher-paying jobs in digital marketing or e-commerce. Furthermore, if you learn a language or gain expertise in a specific field, such as data analysis or project management, you may be able to command a higher salary than your peers who lack these skills.

Personal growth

Acquiring new skills can also lead to personal growth. Learning new skills can broaden your knowledge and perspective, help you develop new interests, and boost your confidence. Additionally, learning new skills can help you stay mentally sharp and active, which can improve your overall well-being and quality of life.

Moreover, learning new skills can help you build new relationships and connections with other people who share your interests. For example, if you're interested in learning a new language, you can join a language-learning group or attend a language class, where you can meet other people who share your interest. This can help you build a network of supportive people who can provide advice, support, and encouragement as you continue to learn and grow.

Better job satisfaction

Acquiring new skills can also lead to better job satisfaction. When you have a diverse range of skills and are continuously learning and growing, you are more likely to be engaged and satisfied with your work. Furthermore, by developing new skills, you may be able to take on new challenges and responsibilities in your job, which can make your work more interesting and fulfilling.

Moreover, having a broader range of skills can make you more versatile and adaptable in your job. This can help you handle unexpected challenges and changes in your work environment, which can be particularly valuable in industries that are rapidly changing or experiencing disruption.

Conclusion

In conclusion, acquiring new skills is essential for personal and professional development. By learning new skills, you can improve your job prospects, increase your earning potential, experience personal growth, and enjoy better job satisfaction. Whether you're interested in learning a new language, developing expertise in a specific field, or gaining new technical skills, the benefits of acquiring new skills are numerous and valuable. By making a commitment to lifelong learning, you can continue to grow and develop throughout your career and life.